# Thankful

Julie Chapus

# Thankful

Inspired by God

Written by Julie Chapus © 2015

ISBN:978-1-935018-97-1

### Scripture

Scripture used in this book is from the NIV unless otherwise noted.

The Holy Bible, New International Version®, NIV® Copyright © 1973, 1978, 1984, 2011 by Biblica, Inc.® Used by permission. All rights reserved worldwide.

Scripture quotations marked (NLT) are taken from the Holy Bible, New Living Translation, copyright © 1996, 2004, 2007 by Tyndale House Foundation. Used by permission of Tyndale House Publishers, Inc., Carol Stream, Illinois 60188. All rights reserved.

Scripture quotations marked (HCSB) are taken from the Holman Christian Standard Bible® Copyright © 1999, 2000, 2002, 2003, 2009 by Holman Bible Publishers. Used with permission by Holman Bible Publishers, Nashville, Tennessee. All rights reserved.

Scripture quotations marked (NKJV) are taken from the New King James Version®. Copyright © 1982 by Thomas Nelson. Used by permission. All rights reserved.

Scripture quotations marked (AMP) are taken from the Amplified® Bible,

Copyright © 1954, 1958, 1962, 1964, 1965, 1987 by The Lockman Foundation

Used by permission.

Christ for Kids
Ministries

# Dedications

This book is dedicated first and foremost to God our Father. Without You Lord, the words on these pages would not have been possible. Thank You so much for sharing Your wisdom with us. May we always be thankful to You, God, for all You do for us, and through us.

Martha Chapus ~ The Lord has given me so much to be thankful for, but one of the greatest blessings is you. I love you.

*~In Remembrance of~*

Aaron Schoffstall, my friend, pen pal, and space camp buddy who always encouraged me and made me laugh. We lost you in a tragic accident, as you were trying to help someone else. I am forever blessed to have had our time together as kids. I am truly honored and thankful to have known you. You are greatly missed but never forgotten!

# Thank You

Thank you, David and Abby for your support. The Lord has given us a tremendous responsibility and I am so thankful we get to serve Him as a family united in Christ.

Thank you to my editors, Jennifer Edwards and David Chapus. Your prayers, patience, fasting, and suggestions always make these books everything the Lord wants them to be. Thank you so much for all of your hard work.

Thank you, Mom, Dad, and Marie for supporting me in all my endeavors.

Thank you, Pastor Joshua Finley for your prayers, help, support, and for believing in me. I am thankful for all the encouragement you have given me over these past few years. It means more to me than you know.

Thank you, Healing and Release teams at both campuses of Elim Gospel Church. Your help was greatly needed and your willingness to serve has helped me tremendously. Thank you!

Thank you, monks at the Abbey of the Genesee. You have provided a very special and safe place for me to write this book and I am always blessed and in awe of the prayer covering and protection at the Abbey. Thank you so much for all you do night and day for all of us.

Thank you, Katie Bebbington, for your prayers and support. May the Oasis prayer room always hold a special place in our hearts!

Thank you, Kathy Durgo, for your time and prayers. May we reach many, that they may know their true identity in Christ.

Thank you, Wegmans supermarkets, for sowing seeds in me that would produce a harvest of good fruit!

Thank you, Judge Michael Telesca, for helping Christ for Kids Ministries reach the nations!

# Table of Contents

Dedications ..................................................................3

Thank You ...................................................................5

Introduction ................................................................9

The Journey ..............................................................11

Soaring Above Attitudes ........................................23

Selfish or Thankful? .................................................33

Practice Doesn't Have to Make Perfect ...............37

Busyness ....................................................................43

Peace in the Quiet ...................................................47

Jesus and the Holy Spirit .......................................51

It's Time To Tell the Truth ....................................57

Peace Stealers ............................................................63

A Gift For You .........................................................69

Conclusion ................................................................75

Suggested Reading List ..........................................81

# Introduction

Have you ever been thankful for something? Perhaps you were once given a pet; wasn't that one of the happiest moments of your life? Do you remember holding that cute fuzzy creature, knowing it was yours to keep, care for, and love?

At times like that it is very easy for us to feel thankful. But what about the bad times, when everything seems to be going wrong? At times like those, it can be very difficult for us to feel thankful for anything.

In this book we are going to learn why God wants us to be thankful for everything in our lives, even for things that seem bad. It may be hard to be thankful for things we don't like or want in our lives, but we will discover why this is good for us and for those around us. Most importantly, we will learn how to do this God's way. If you are ready, let's turn the page and go on this journey together.

# The Journey

This journey begins a few years ago, in my kitchen. One day I made a batch of lemonade for my family. I put it in a glass pitcher and stuck it in the fridge. When it was time to serve the lemonade, I opened the refrigerator door, and you would not believe the mess I saw. My glass pitcher had exploded; I mean it looked as if it had blown up! There was shattered glass and lemonade everywhere. I have no idea how or why my pitcher blew up, but it did.

Not only was there was a huge mess to clean up, but I had to throw out almost everything in the refrigerator, because tiny pieces of glass had gotten into much of the food. As you can imagine, I was not happy about this. It took me hours to clean that fridge. Because of all the shattered glass, I had to be careful so I wouldn't get cut. And of course I couldn't just use plain water, since the lemonade was sticky. I had to use hot soapy water, and scrub to get the stickiness off the shelves, drawers, and door. That was one of the worst messes I had ever cleaned in a kitchen.

Naturally, I was pretty frustrated over the whole ordeal. My husband was not home, and my daughter was too young to help, so I had to clean up this mess all by myself. I can assure you, at the time I was not thanking God for any of this. Instead, I was complaining and grumbling all the while I was cleaning the fridge. After what seemed like hours of work, the fridge finally looked clean again.

A few weeks after this incident, the Lord put it on our family's hearts to move to a different home. This was sudden and surprising, but we obeyed God, and bought the house God wanted us to move into.

We began the tough job of packing up our belongings in the old house. There was so much to do. If you have ever moved, you know how hard it can be. We had to go through every room and decide what to take, what to give away, and what to throw out. It was a very tiring process.

Finally, it was moving day. The last thing we had left to pack was the food in our kitchen. I was so tired and exhausted from all the packing and moving heavy boxes, by the time I walked into that kitchen I just wanted to collapse. I opened the refrigerator door and to my surprise it still looked like new! At that moment, I was so happy and thankful the lemonade pitcher had exploded when it did, because I just didn't have it in me to clean or pack one more thing. We were able to just focus on moving to the new house, and I didn't have to worry about cleaning out the fridge. It was like finding an oasis in the middle of the desert of packing. It was a major relief.

The point of sharing this story is to show how things happen that we may find unpleasant, and we are not always happy about them; yet they can turn out to be a huge help and a blessing to us. We may not understand why things happen at the time, but God has a plan for us, and when the time is right, He will show us and give us exactly what we need to come out of hardships and problems trusting Him.

In the Bible Ecclesiastes 8:6 states, *"For there is a proper time and procedure for every matter, though a person may be weighed down by misery."*

God knew the perfect time for me to tackle that fridge was before the move. I remember opening that refrigerator door on moving day and saying, "Thank You God! I am so happy that pitcher exploded when it did, because I don't have it in me to clean one more thing!" I knew then that God had used something bad (my exploding lemonade pitcher), and He turned it into something good. From then on, I also started taking a little more seriously God's words about being thankful.

What words am I talking about? Well, the Bible (God's Word) tells us to *"give thanks in all circumstances, for this is God's will for you in Christ Jesus."* (1 Thessalonians 5:18)

I used to give thanks only when things were going my way. When I didn't get my way, I would be very upset, and even blame God for not giving me the things I wanted. This was such an issue for me, I have written a whole book about this topic, called *The Blame Game*.

It took me years to learn that I needed to give thanks to God always, even when things seem to be bad. It does not feel natural to be thankful during bad times, but I learned God will make something good come out of it, in His own time. This was a very hard lesson for me to learn, though, and it took me a long time to actually put thankfulness into practice.

Growing up, my parents took us to church every Sunday. I thought going to church was a duty. I looked at going to church as a way to make God happy. And I figured that after church, we could just live however we felt like living, and we could do whatever we wanted to. I wouldn't even think about God again until the next Sunday, when it was time for church again.

I had no clue back then that God really wants to be in the middle of our lives every single day, and not just on Sundays. I also had no idea He wants to have a real relationship with us. I thought going to church on Sundays was all we needed to do. I didn't know that God created us with a specific plan in mind and that we should be turning to Him every day of our lives.

It's important to share this with you, because for years and years I suffered from fear, anxiety, stress, and a lot of bad feelings. You name the emotion, I had a problem with it. I cannot imagine how different my life could have been if only I had known God's Word in the Bible. If I had prayed to God, and learned the truth about the kind of relationship He wants to have with us, I can honestly tell you I would have lived a lot differently.

The Bible Ephesians 2:10 tells us, *"For we are God's handiwork, created in Christ Jesus to do good works, which God prepared in advance for us to do."* So when God created us, He had a plan in mind for each of us.

We are all on a journey called life, and we can either try to figure it all out on our own, or we can ask God to help us by leading us down the paths He has created for us.

Pastor Josh at the church I now attend, Elim Gospel Church, once put it this way: "You are a living, breathing solution to a problem in our world. When God created you, He made every detail about you, right down to your personality. Everything about you is God's creative solution to a problem in our world. If you do not step into the plans God has for you, no one else will, because no else was created just like you. There is only one of you, and if you don't do what God created you for, no one else can, because no one else was created for that exact purpose and that exact plan."

Amazing, isn't it? But is it really true? Are we really loved, cared for and created for a specific, unique purpose? God's Word says Yes! The Apostle Paul asks the question, *"Has God rejected and disowned His people?"* He then gives us the answer: *"No, God has not rejected his own people, whom he chose from the very beginning."* (Romans 11 NLT)

The Bible also says *"My frame was not hidden from you [God] when I was made in the secret place, when I was woven together in the depths of the earth. Your eyes saw my unformed body; all the days ordained for me were written in your book before one of them came to be."* (Psalm 139:15-16)

The book of Jeremiah says, *"I chose you before I formed you in the womb; I set you apart before you were born. I appointed you a prophet to the nations."* (Jeremiah 1:5 HCSB)

Romans likewise states, *"For God knew his people in advance, and he chose them to be like his Son, so that his Son would be the firstborn among many brothers and sisters."* (Romans 8:29 NLT)

We have so many examples in the Bible of God creating us for a plan and a purpose and loving us before we were even born! If only I had known this information when I was younger. I tried figuring out everything on my own for years. I tried to plan what I should do and be when I grew up, I tried to fit in with the crowd, and I chased after love and approval, not realizing God already loved and approved of me.

After years spent chasing after all the wrong things, I can tell you, it's far better just to turn to God. He knows the plan for each of our lives, and He helps us discover that plan. Others may try to help us, but God is the only true planner.

There is a saying people often tell kids to try to encourage them; perhaps someone has said it to you: "You can be anything you want to be."

A lot of parents say this to their kids; so do teachers. It was told to me when I was younger, and I've heard it said on TV. But will we really be happy, and have peace in our hearts, if what we are doing is not God's plan for us?

See, this saying taught me that I should go after what I wanted; it didn't tell me that God already had a plan for me. This saying taught me to focus on myself and not on God. It would have been much better had someone told me, "You can be everything God created you to be." That would have helped me turn to God, instead of spending years chasing after what I wanted to do.

So what's wrong with doing what you want to? Well, when God created us He put in us certain gifts and abilities to carry out the purpose we were created for. When we are not living the life we were created for, we won't have peace and we will not be fulfilled.

We often think our plans will lead us to peace and happiness, and that is why we choose our own way. We come up with bright ideas that we think will be good for us, but when they turn out badly, and we realize we missed the mark, we start all over, thinking, "OK, maybe I'll try this or that instead." It's exhausting trying to figure out our life on our own. But it does not have to be that way. The problem is, most of us don't even know there is another way. That is the reason why I spent years chasing after things I thought would make me happy, only to end up feeling miserable.

When I was young, my dream was to be an astronaut. I loved space, I loved anything that had to do with flying, and like a lot of kids I dreamed of someday going into space, maybe even to the moon. So I went to space camp and space academy, and I learned everything I could about becoming an astronaut. It was a lot of fun for me. I met some awesome friends, including Aaron Schoffstall, to whom this book is dedicated. We attended space camp together, and he was my pen pal for years afterward. I also got to meet a real astronaut, Eileen Collins. Going to camp and learning about space was a great experience for me. I thought, for sure this is for me!

As I got older, I continued to pursue my goal. When I became a young adult I took lessons on how to fly sailplanes. I figured if I could do that, I would be on my way to flying rocket ships one day. These were all good, enjoyable experiences for me, but the problem was, none of this was God's plan for my life.

Sure, I learned a lot, and I had fun doing it, but as I headed to college, I realized that if I was really going to try to become an astronaut, I had to start getting serious about aerospace and aeronautics. So I started taking courses in physics, computer science, math, and aviation.

And you know what? I wasn't good at any of them. In fact, I failed them all! I was stressed out all the time; I didn't know what to do. My dream, the plan I had, the plan I believed in, was falling apart, and there was nothing I could do to fix it. I think many of us are like that; a lot of people spend years in school and jobs, chasing after what they want, only to realize they don't like what they are doing once they get there.

But God did not create you or me to be miserable. Some people figure, "Well, I've spent all this time and money to go to school for this, I may as well just do it," but they hate what they are doing. They end up unhappy, severely depressed or worse, lost. Feeling as if they have no purpose at all.

The Bible John 10:10 states, *"The thief comes only to steal and kill and destroy; I have come that they may have life, and have it to the full."* The plans we make are sometimes like the thief; they take away all the peace and joy that could be ours. They steal the deep inner satisfaction we get from doing what we were created for.

When we only follow our own plans, without considering what God wants us to do, we often end up feeling inadequate, dissatisfied, and frustrated. We would never imagine doing on our own what God created us to do. He created us to do some powerful things in our world. He created us to be world changers, but we cannot do these things without God's help. What often happens is, we become so focused on what we want (or what we think we want), and get so wrapped up in trying to figure things out on our own, we completely forget about God and His plans for us.

It's sad to look back and see chunks of our lives stolen from us, simply because we didn't realize we could have turned to God in the first place. But let's not despair! God still has a plan and purpose for us, and it's never too late to follow that plan, no matter how old you are or how many mistakes you've made. Did you know Moses, one of the greatest heroes of the Bible, was 80 years old when he did his most important work God had planned for him? So it's true, we are never too old! The Bible tells us in Romans 11:29 (AMP), *"For God's gifts and His call are irrevocable. He never withdraws them when once they are given, and He does not change His mind about those to whom He gives His grace or to whom He sends His call."* This is great news for all of us!

When we focus only on ourselves and on our plans and what we want, we will be robbing ourselves of the awesome plan God has for us and the peace and joy God wants us to have right now! Understanding this simple truth can tremendously help us in our lives.

You may be wondering, well, is it even good for us to come up with plans and set goals for ourselves in the first place? Yes, but the key is turning to God first and foremost. Once we invite God into our hearts, and ask Him to help us live out the life He created us for, setting goals and having a plan can be very helpful. It's important for us to have a plan on how to accomplish the tasks God has given us. For instance, I know it is God's plan for me to write books for young people, so when I sit down to write, I set a schedule and do what I can in that time frame each day.

God has also given me a family, though, so I still have my responsibilities as a wife and mom. I need to plan out my day so that I will have time to write, without neglecting my family. God wants me taking good care of everything He has given me, the books as well as my family. I can't ignore important areas of my life and let my child go hungry because I am too busy writing. Having a goal and plan in mind allows me to accomplish everything God wants me doing. But the important thing for me is to take the time to allow God to point me in the right direction first.

Do you know, I have no idea what to write about on my own? It's true! God is the one who gives me the titles of these books and it's only when I spend time with Him that He tells me what to put in the books. Only God will make our paths straight and help us accomplish all He has given us to do. He will help us discover what the next step is.

If you are ready to take that next step into everything God has planned for you, let's turn to God and ask Him to help you live your life according to His plan. Here's a prayer to help.

### Prayer

*Dear God, thank You for creating me with a plan in mind. I don't want to spend years chasing all the wrong goals, God. Please open my heart and show me what You want me to do. Lead me and guide me in the way I should go. Dear God, I want to be everything You created me to be. Amen.*

\* \* \* \*

Before we move on, I'd like to say a few words about—and to—parents.

What if we want to live out God's plans for our life, but our parents already have a plan in mind for us? What should we do then?

First, don't be worried. The Lord knows your heart, and He wants to help. Just tell God that you want to live according to His plan for your life. He will make that happen, no matter what situation you are in. The Bible Jeremiah 29:11 tells us: *"For I know the plans I have for you, declares the Lord; plans to prosper you and not to harm you, plans to give you hope and a future."* Here is a prayer you may find helpful, if you are facing this kind of situation.

### Prayer

*Dear God, please help me to live out the plans You have for my life. Please help my parents too. Soften their hearts, so that they may accept Your plan for my life. Thank you, God. I am trusting You. Amen.*

While it's most important that we turn to God first, it's also a good idea to speak openly to our parents about our concerns. Sometimes it can be difficult to know how to express our feelings, or where to begin. So the following discussion is written for parents. If you're struggling with a conflict between what you believe God's plan is for your life, and what your parents have in mind for you, ask them to read this section. Better yet, read it with them and discuss it together.

Parents: How do we as parents allow our kids to be all God created them to be? Some of us want so badly to have kids, and to see them become successful, that when our children are born, we have their whole lives planned out for them. We know what college we would like them to attend. We envision them going into certain careers, we tell them what sports they will play, and even what cars they will drive. Many well-meaning parents do this because we want what's best for our children. We don't want our kids to struggle in life the way we did. Many parents think, if my kid can get into this or that career, he or she will be set for life.

These are powerful motivations, with a well-intentioned desire to help our children. It is usually out of good intentions that we parents put this added pressure on our kids. But if our plans for our children are not consistent with God's plans, our children's peace and joy will be stolen from them. None of us want that. We want our children to be well physically, mentally, emotionally, and spiritually. That is true success.

As a parent, it has been helpful for me to look at our Heavenly Father as an example. When I think about God, I realize He does not force any of us into His plans. He allows us to choose the way we want to live, even when He knows we are making bad choices, and He patiently waits for us to return to Him.

That is exactly what God did in my life. He did not force me into anything; He waited for me to turn to Him. If God, our Heavenly Father, treats us this way, shouldn't we as parents do the same with our children?

The Bible tells us to, *"Teach a youth about the way he should go, even when he is old he will not depart from it."* (Proverbs 22:6 HCSB)

So perhaps instead of trying to force our wills on our children, we can teach them to turn to God instead. Once our kids are in God's hands, we can trust and know they will be fulfilled and at peace, because they will be in the hands of the One who created them, for a purpose known best to Him.

Putting these lessons into practice is not always going to be easy. It's hard to cede control over our children's lives, even to God. Here are some prayers that you may find helpful.

*Prayer*

*Dear Lord, please help me trust You as I place my child in your hands. I love and appreciate the child You have given me, but I know ultimately he/she is Yours, and was created for Your purposes. Help me to steward my child(ren) during my short time as a parent, and help me lead my child(ren) to You. Amen.*

*Prayer*

*Dear God, forgive me for only living my own way, and for forcing my way on others. I want to be the person You created me to be. Please help me turn to You with all my heart, and help me live out the plan You have for my life. Help my children live the life you have for them too. Thank you for showing us the way we should go, Lord. Amen.*

Let's also take a moment to thank the Lord for all He has given us, and for creating us with a special plan and purpose in mind.

*Prayer*

*Thank You, God, for all You have done for us, and for all You wish to accomplish through us, and for the child(ren) you have given us. We thank You for being a good and faithful Father. Amen.*

# Soaring Above Attitudes

Flying sailplanes (sometimes called gliders) is also known as soaring. It is different from flying conventional planes, because sailplanes do not have engines. That makes them extremely quiet. When a sailplane is in the air, the only sound the pilot hears is the wind.

I took up soaring because I thought it would help me achieve my plan of becoming an astronaut, but I came to love soaring for its own sake. When I was in the air I felt a great sense of calm and peace. So my attitude toward soaring soon switched from seeing it as a means of achieving a goal (becoming an astronaut) to using it to try to escape from my problems.

High school was not a pleasant experience for me. I always seemed to have some kind of problem, either with my classes or with other students. I was stressed out about something nearly every day. But when I would get into a sailplane, I pushed aside all the things that were bothering me. I tore into the wind, and the wind carried me and my problems away.

The problem with this was that as soon as I landed, my problems were still there. I didn't have a personal relationship with God yet, and I knew almost nothing about the Bible, so I didn't realize that trying to escape my problems was not going to solve them. I just knew that for a few hours, I didn't have to think about my problems.

So I started to believe that I could just get away from anything that was bothering me, by getting into a glider. Soaring became a temporary escape from my problems.

This thinking was not healthy though. As much as I may have wanted to, I couldn't escape my problems forever. Even though I felt at peace when I was soaring, sooner or later I had to land. I couldn't live up there in the soundless clouds. I needed to eat, I needed to sleep, I needed to go to school, and I needed to live on planet Earth with other people. I couldn't do all of those things in a sailplane.

Many of us use temporary escapes to avoid anxiety or difficult situations. Some turn to harmful activities such as substance abuse or smoking or overeating. Some forms of escape may even seem beneficial, like exercising, or in my case flying. But when we overuse anything to avoid our problems, or neglect life by focusing on our escape strategy, we can easily become lost.

Eventually I had to stop flying, because when I started college, I no longer had the time to fly. My stress and anxiety continued to increase, as did my unhealthy beliefs about needing to escape my problems. To make matters worse, the desire to find some way out of my problems led me to become involved in a dangerous and emotionally abusive relationship. I was believing empty promises from a boyfriend instead of God's biblical truths.

This was all very unhealthy and I really lost the sense of who I was. In short, my life had become a total mess, and it wasn't getting any better.

At that point, I thought everything in my life was hopeless. I felt bad about myself, and what peace I thought I had, no longer existed. Soaring was no longer an option. I was increasingly adding new responsibilities with less and less solid ground to stand on. It was like carrying more and more baggage on thin ice that was cracking beneath me.

I didn't know where to turn, and things were looking pretty bleak. I was failing every class I needed to become an astronaut, and God was still not on my radar screen. But, thank God, I was on His!

God always has us on His radar. No matter what kind of stress we are going through, no matter how bad our life may seem, God sees us.

He knows us and He loves us. If you are feeling hopeless and have not found the words to say to God, let's do this together. Here is a prayer to help.

### Prayer

> *Dear God, thank You for knowing me and loving me. I need You, Lord. Please enter my heart and life. Lead me in the way You want me to go. When I feel like a mess and I cannot see the way forward, You do, Lord, and I am trusting You to guide me. I don't want to live my life without You. I need Your help every day. Thank You for helping me, Lord. I love You. Amen.*

Now when I was going through all these problems, I did not say that prayer, or anything like it, because I still didn't know God. But God can and will use anything to grab our attention. It may be an event in our lives, or it may be another person.

In my case, it was a person who started talking to me one day about God. That was the turning point for me. After our conversation I decided I needed God in my life.

But while that was an important step for me, I also made a significant mistake. Instead of turning only to God as in the prayer above, I turned instead to the person who had told me about God. I began believing she had all the answers to my problems. Once again I was believing my own faulty thinking. I figured, well, this person knows God, and I really don't. I didn't trust myself to make good decisions, so I just accepted whatever she told me. I didn't consult God's word to see if what she told me was His truth. I took what seemed like truth, because it was better than how I was living, and I simply applied those teachings to my life. So once again I was placing my faith and hope in someone else, and it led to more problems in my life.

I truly did want to please God, and I did want a relationship with Him. I just didn't know how to go about it. I still had very little idea or understanding of the truths in the Bible, so I went with what was told to me, and that led me to believe half-truths and lies.

But God loves us so much, He will use whatever He can to bring us into a relationship with Him, even if we have been led astray by others, or by our own false thinking. God will use it to bring us closer to Him. And that's what happened with me.

Eventually I started praying to God every morning, and that is where my relationship with God truly began. For a while, though, I continued to depend more on people than on God to lead me and guide me. Slowly but surely, though, God was teaching me. The more I turned to Him, the better off I was.

This did not happen overnight; it took me years to get over the false belief that my relationship with God depended on other people. I saw other people as a window to God, but in reality they were more like a barrier. I thought that if other people didn't like me or were not pleased with me, God must feel the same way.

That was a terrible lie, faulty thinking, and a horrible burden to live under. It caused me to live in a constant state of fear and anxiety. I can see now that I really didn't know God, I only knew Him through the lens of another person, and I had no idea just how much God really does love us.

Think of someone you know really well, like your sister or brother or a good friend. You know what they like and don't like, you probably even know how they will react to certain situations. Now let's say you hear about someone you have never met. You really have no idea about this person's personality or what they like and don't like. You only know what someone else told you about them, and you can't even be sure if it's true without meeting the person yourself. You would never say you knew somebody that you had only heard things about.

It's no wonder, then, that temporary escapes and other people are not the answer to our problems. When we live with so much fear, anxiety, loneliness and despair, no plane ride or any other distraction or person can ever make those feelings go away for good. Only God can do that. God wants to help us overcome our problems.

The reason I am sharing this with you is that I don't want you to make the same mistakes I made. Other people may love us and have very good intentions for us, but they, like us, are still imperfect. We all make mistakes and have flaws. Only God is perfect. People do not know all the things God created us to do. Only He knows the whole plan for our life. So looking to other people to guide us and tell us what we should do with our lives can be very damaging, especially when we take their advice over God's. Our only true help and peace comes when we turn to God. Only He can cast out fear, loneliness, anxiety and any other negative emotions we may be having.

If you can relate to this, let's say a prayer right now to return us to the truth.

### Prayer

*Dear God, please forgive me for putting other people in Your place. You are the only one true God. It is You who created me, and I know You love me. Please lead me and guide me in the way I should go. Give me the courage to seek You only and to turn away from anything in my life that is not pleasing to You. I want to live according to Your plan for my life. I cannot do this without You, Lord! Amen.*

Of course, saying this prayer will not make all our problems magically go away. Our lives do not become problem-free the second we turn to God. And God does not promise us a problem-free life. He does promise to never leave us or forsake us. He is our ever-present help in trouble. Psalm 46:1 states, *"God is our refuge and strength, an ever present help in trouble."*

God will see us through our problems. And when we get past the troubled areas of our lives, we can look back and clearly see what God did to help us, and those around us. God is always ready to help us grow closer to Him. We can be very thankful for that. The closer we get to God, the more peace we have inside us, because we truly know we are never alone!

These are all lessons I have learned, but it took me a long time—years, in fact. Even as I was beginning to draw closer to God, I still had some bad attitudes and faulty beliefs that God needed to help me with, and I still wanted things to go my way. But even though I was continuing to hold onto wrong thoughts and beliefs, God was helping me anyway. He did not allow my faults and failures to affect His plans for my life.

It's amazing to me to think about how God really does care about us, even when we don't know Him or think about Him. He is still watching over all of us, always.

Here is another example where God was working in my life, even before I truly knew Him.

While I was in college, I landed a job as a photo lab technician at Wegmans supermarkets to help me pay for my books and supplies. Although I had a lot of problems in school, I liked my job at Wegmans; it was fun, and I learned a lot while I was there.

Wegmans also had a college scholarship program that student employees could apply for. I decided to apply, but I was not hopeful at all. My dream of becoming an astronaut was falling apart before my eyes. I felt like a failure. I didn't see any value in myself, and I had very low self-esteem. But I figured I had nothing to lose by applying for the scholarship, so I did.

As part of my application, I had to write an essay. I didn't think much of my writing. So imagine my surprise when Wegmans informed me I had won a scholarship. I couldn't believe it!

I was unaware of it at the time, but God was using Wegmans to sow seeds in me, that would grow and bear fruit later on. Winning that scholarship wasn't just about money for me. It planted the realization in me that someone saw something of value in me. Someone believed in me so much that they wanted to give me money to go to college!

Wegmans saw something in me that I hadn't seen in myself. Their attitude was, let's send this girl to school so she can help make our world a better place! I wouldn't have been able to imagine back then that anyone would even want to read anything that I wrote, much less that they would like it. I certainly had no idea that God would eventually upgrade my life from writing essays for a scholarship application, to writing entire books all about Him!

So you see, God is always working, whether we are aware of Him or not. He is always using the things around us to try to get our attention. Even if it takes years, it is worth it, because God loves us so much and He will make things work out for us!

Once I entered into a relationship with God, I began to see positive changes happening in my life. I was experiencing more and more peace, as I learned to turn to God and His ways. I also started spending more time with God. I read my Bible daily, and turned God's Word into prayers. The more I prayed, the more peace I started to feel. Do you know what I finally learned? All those years when I was trying to escape my problems by soaring, I could have had peace without ever needing to leave the ground or turn to anything or anyone else!

Soaring was great, but I realize now that I didn't have to keep trying to escape my problems. God was showing me as our relationship grew that He was with me, and He was the reason I experienced peace.

Once we realize we are not alone, and that we are not expected to solve all our problems on our own, our stress just seems to vanish. We no longer feel all that pressure to be perfect. I didn't have to keep feeling bad about my faults and failures. All I had to do was rest in the fact that God is perfect, and He is the one who helps me do what needs to be done. I am not expected to do anything on my own. In fact, the Bible clearly states that we can't do anything apart from God: *"I am the vine, you are the branches. He who abides in me and I in him bears much fruit, for without Me you can do nothing."* (John 15:5 NKJV)

God is the only one who makes the impossible, possible. The Bible states, *"But Jesus looked at them and said, 'With man this is impossible, but with God all things are possible.'"* (Matthew 19:26) Turning to our Bible will pour truth into our lives and teach us how to handle our problems God's ways.

One of the most valuable lessons I have learned is not just to read the Bible, but to turn the words of the Bible into prayers. Here is an example of turning scripture into prayer.

Philippians 4:6-7 says, *"Do not be anxious about anything, but in every situation by prayer and petition with thanksgiving present your requests to God. And the peace of God which transcends all understanding will guard your hearts and your minds in Christ Jesus."* So let's use that to come up with a prayer.

### Prayer

*Dear Lord, help me not to be anxious about anything. Help me remember to pray, and be thankful to You for everything. Help me turn to You in all my circumstances. Please give me Your peace, which transcends all understanding. Guard my heart and my mind in Christ Jesus. Amen.*

Now that was just an example. There is no right or wrong way to do this. Just take a passage from the Bible that you find especially meaningful and turn it into a prayer. It's easy!

Doing this helps us turn to God even more, and to pray for things we might not have thought of on our own. When I read the above scripture, what stood out to me was that word thanksgiving. Although I was growing closer to God at that time in my life, and doing more things His way, I still hadn't taken God's words fully to heart, especially where thankfulness was concerned. I tried to do what the Bible said about praying to God, and I also did the petition part, asking God for help, but I didn't do the part about being thankful. The only time I ever thanked God was when I got my way. The attitude in my heart was not a thankful one.

God had to help me understand that giving thanks means we should thank Him when we get our way and when we don't! We're supposed to be thankful to God all the time, no matter what.

As I said, I was very slow to learn this. It has taken me years to put this lesson into practice on a daily basis. Remember the lemonade? It's hard to thank God in all situations, especially when problems arise. But after that experience, I decided it was time for me to start.

Thanking God for everything, even the unpleasant things, will give us peace. No one likes or wants problems, of course, but the more we thank God, the more we experience peace. With more peace we begin to better understand that we are going to be all right in any situation. When we experience God's peace, we know for sure we are not alone. We believe and know God is going to help us, and that will always make us feel calmer inside.

The Lord helped me to understand the passage in Philippians 4:7 where it says, *"The peace of God which transcends all understanding will guard your hearts and your minds in Christ Jesus."* And I've learned that we can experience that peace even though we may have many problems to deal with. When we follow this scripture completely, by praying, asking God for what we need, and thanking Him no matter how bad things may seem, God will give us a greater sense of peace than we can imagine or understand; it transcends understanding.

When we're in the middle of a difficult situation, this may not seem to make any sense at all. We may wonder, "How can I possibly have peace while I'm in this mess?" The answer is, God is going to give us peace, because it is He who is guarding our hearts and minds to help us get through whatever it is, and He will give us what we need. He is the superhero that comes to our rescue. He shields us, covers us, and cloaks us. We do not have to be afraid. To put it another way, do not fear, Jesus is here!

**Prayer**

*Dear God, please help me with this (state your problem). Grant me peace, and the tools that I need to get through this according to Your way. Help me to be thankful for what is happening. I know You are in control and I want to handle this in a way that honors You. Thank You so much, God, for all You are doing. I know You have an awesome plan for me. Amen.*

# Selfish or Thankful?

One of the most famous lines in history was written over 400 years ago by the great playwright William Shakespeare, in his play *Hamlet*: "To be, or not to be, that is the question." When Shakespeare wrote that line, the character in the play was talking about life and death. But we can also apply his question to our attitudes: "To be thankful or not to be thankful, that is the question." Which do you choose?

Why does this question matter? Let's explore. Most of us know how good it feels to get exactly what we want. Has there ever been a time when you were hoping and wishing for one particular thing you really wanted, and then you got it? It's an awesome feeling, right?

But of course, we don't always get what we want. And we all know what that feels like too. When we have our heart set on something, and we don't get it, that can hurt. It makes us unhappy. It's downright depressing.

So we shouldn't depend on getting things to make us feel happy. But did you know we can choose to feel happy, whether we get what we want or not? It's true—it's called joy! How do we get that? By giving thanks in those tough times!

Is this for real? Just bear with me—I promise it will make sense. Let's do an experiment together. Think of something you'd really like to have. Maybe it's some kind of toy or game. It may not be a physical thing; for example, it might be a vacation to some particular place, or attending some event. You know you don't have this thing, but you would very much like to have it.

Now let's say you're told that you will never get that thing. How would that make you feel? Most likely, not very good! But don't worry, the next part of this experiment will cheer us up!

Now think of something you already have; something you really love. Perhaps it's a stuffed animal or maybe a pet, or a parent; it could be almost anything. Now say, "Thank you, God, for giving me this." Take a moment to let that thought sink in. Let your heart become full of thanks. It feels good, doesn't it? What that shows is that simply changing our way of thinking from focusing on what we don't have, to being happy for what we do have, helps us feel much better.

This also shows us how powerful our thoughts are! Our thoughts have the ability to change our moods and our feelings. This took me years to learn and it is important to share, because just by giving thanks, our entire perspective on our lives can change completely.

The great thing about this is that we don't need to have a lot of material things in order to be thankful. We can all think of something in our lives we are thankful for. Probably many things, in fact. Are you healthy? Then thank God for your health! We can thank God for clean water, for food, for our families, our homes ... I'm sure you can think of a lot of things to be thankful for in your life, too.

Psalm 119:62 states, *"At midnight I rise to give you thanks for your righteous laws."* We don't have to do it at midnight, but we can wake up every day and say, "Thank you, God, for your words in the Bible!" God's words help us every day. The truth is that when we are thankful, our hearts grow more peaceful. We feel satisfied and joyful when we give thanks to God.

But when we are selfish and think of only what we don't have and what we wish we had, our hearts lose peace, and the feeling of being satisfied and joyful disappears. We become sad and begin to search for things to fill us back up emotionally. When we choose not to be thankful, we feel miserable, and it leads to frustration. We go through all kinds of effort to get what we think we want. It can become a very tiring cycle, and it shifts our focus away from the good things in our lives to what we lack. It always leads to a slew of bad emotions. We may feel as if we will never have enough, and that worse yet, no one cares—which we know is untrue. Being thankful safeguards our hearts and minds and gives us joy.

Remember, being thankful is a choice that any of us can make. We do not have to wait for a special feeling to come to us. We don't have to wait until we "get" something either. We can choose right here and now to be thankful for the blessings we already have in our lives. This will help us grow the peace in our hearts that God wants us to have, and it will also remind us just how much we really are loved by God.

Here are some scriptures from the Bible that may be helpful in reinforcing these lessons. Remember, we can also turn these scriptures into prayers, just as we did before.

Psalm 100:4: *"Enter his gates with thanksgiving, and his courts with praise; give thanks to him and praise his name."*

Psalm 119:36: *"Turn my heart toward your statutes and not toward selfish gain."*

Ephesians 5:19: *"Speaking to one another with psalms, hymns, and songs from the Spirit, sing and make music from your heart to the Lord, always giving thanks to God the Father for everything in the name of our Lord Jesus Christ."*

If we turn to God and take His Word into our hearts and minds by reading and praying the Bible every day, it will help us immensely. And if we are struggling with selfishness and having a hard time being thankful, God's Word will make things better. His Word really does help us and heal us, even from our own thoughts, moods, and emotions.

My deepest and sincerest prayer is that we will be able to answer William Shakespeare's age-old question with, "I choose to be thankful!" Here's a prayer to help.

**Prayer**

*Dear God, please help me choose to live a thankful life. Help me do what Your Word says and give thanks, even when I am not getting my way. Change my heart, Lord, so that I can choose to follow Your ways over mine. Thank You for always reminding me that I can be thankful for You every day. Amen*

# Practice Doesn't Have to Make Perfect

Have you ever heard the phrase, "practice makes perfect"? Perhaps you play a musical instrument. When you know you have a lesson coming up, do you practice before you go see your teacher? Most of us would, because we want to move forward. We don't want to get stuck doing the same song over and over again and never making any progress. We want to learn new things and keep moving on and getting better. We don't want to keep playing *"Mary Had A Little Lamb"* all our lives.

Well, we can apply practice to our spiritual life too. God has given us many teachings in the Bible that we can practice. One of them includes being thankful. The Bible helps us deal with any problems we may run into, by guiding us and teaching us what we should do. When we don't put God's ways into practice, we usually end up trying to do things our own way. Kind of like when a child taps a piano keyboard with only one finger. It seems fun at the time, and they may enjoy playing the keyboard in their own way, but without instruction and practice, they would never learn to go beyond that, and how to play beautiful music.

When we don't learn new ways, and just do the same old thing over and over, we begin to feel depressed and anxious. We may start to have faulty thoughts, like "Maybe I'm just not good enough. Maybe this is all I can do." Doing the same old thing over and over will never lead us to learn something new. It only gets us stuck in stress, panic and anxiety.

Is the Bible really our answer though? After all, some of us read the Bible every day yet still suffer from wrong thoughts and harmful attitudes. Why is that? The answer is quite simple: while we may read the Bible, we don't always do what the Bible tells us to do. In other words, we don't put it into practice.

James 1:22- 25 says, *"Do not merely listen to the word, and so deceive yourselves. Do what it says. Anyone who listens to the word but does not do what it says is like someone who looks at his face in a mirror, and after looking at himself, goes away and immediately forgets what he looks like. But whoever looks intently into the perfect law [God's Word] that gives freedom and continues in it, not forgetting what they have heard, but doing it, they will be blessed in what they do."*

So if we simply read the Bible, but don't put it into practice, we won't see any good or blessings come from it. In the same way, a musician can read a sheet of music, but if she doesn't actually play it, she won't be making any music at all. And even if she does play it, she will likely need to practice it in order to play it well. If we play an instrument, we cannot expect to pick up a new piece of music, sit down and play it perfectly the first time. We need to keep revisiting the music, and practice it over and over until we get it. This is true for the Bible as well; we have to practice living according to what the Bible says for it to truly become a way of life.

When I started reading the Bible regularly, I began to put some of it into practice, but it took me a long time to learn to be thankful for everything God has done for me, because I didn't practice being thankful. Sometimes I would try to remember to be thankful, for a while, but then I would become distracted by other things and stop practicing.

Just like playing music, when we stop practicing for a while, we may forget what we have learned. Then we will have to re-learn it and start all over again. It can take quite a while to get back into the swing of things.

Practicing anything doesn't always come to us naturally. Doing something over and over again may go against our instincts or our desires. That's why we need to purposely make time for practice. We have to intentionally choose to practice if we want it to become a habit. It can be easy to blow off practice, because we're tired, or just not motivated, or something else comes up that we'd rather be doing.

As I explained earlier, it took me years to really understand that I needed to put the words in the Bible into practice. It was so easy for me to complain about things and to find fault with people. That felt like a natural thing for me to do, but that is not what God's Word tells us to do. If you can relate to this, let's turn to God in prayer.

**Prayer**

*Dear God, please help me put Your words in the Bible into practice. May I make Your Word a priority in my life. Please help me, Lord, to spend time with You every single day. Thank you, Jesus. Amen.*

The Bible tells us to *"do everything without complaining and arguing."* (Philippians 2:14 NLT) I used to think the reason behind that scripture was simply that complaining and arguing is just not helpful.

That's true, but I've since learned that there's more to it than that. God tells us not to complain because complaining about things actually harms us! How? Complaining steals our peace. Faulty thoughts and behaviors like complaining, grumbling and arguing all take our focus off God and onto our personal grudges and dislikes. We can spend all day stewing over things that annoy us, and complaining about this and that, and by the time the day is over, we are exhausted, stressed out, and wondering why we feel so miserable.

I didn't realize what a problem my complaining was until I started to practice being thankful. Remember how thankfulness helps us avoid selfishness? Well, it helps us avoid complaining too. God knows that thankfulness does not always come naturally to us. However, it is God's will for us to be thankful, because He knows that when we are thankful, it will give us a tremendous amount of peace and rest. Remember what the Bible says: *"Give thanks in all circumstances, for this is God's will for you in Christ Jesus."* (1 Thessalonians 5:18) All those years I spent complaining about things, I could have had such a greater level of peace in my heart, and less stress, if I had just practiced that teaching.

It is in my heart to share this with you. I don't want you to go on always wondering what's wrong with your life, or thinking you will never be calm inside, or that there is something wrong with you. God created you, He loves you and He has a good plan to give all of us peace. We just need to turn to Him and learn to put His words into practice.

Now it's important to know that God does not expect us to be perfect. (Thank You, God!) He also does not love us any more or any less based on how well we do. We don't earn brownie points for reading the Bible and we can't earn more love from God, no matter how much we practice. God already loves us, more than we can imagine, because He is our Father—our dad. He created us and there is nothing we could ever do to make God stop loving us. So please don't misunderstand: practicing God's teaching does not equal more love from God.

Practicing is also not something we do for God's benefit. Practicing does not help God, it helps us. He is already perfect. He is trying to help us develop into everything He created us to be. He wants us to have peace in our lives. So practicing His ways is for us only. Whenever we do what God tells us to do, it always helps us. We should never do these things because we think God is going to be mad at us if we don't, or believe the lie that He won't love us anymore if we aren't perfect. It does not benefit God in any way whether we read our Bible or not. God does not need our help, we need His!

Following God benefits us. And practicing His ways helps us better understand Him. God's word shows us just how much He loves us, and learning His ways will always give us more peace, more calm, and lead us to trust Him. He really does know what we need!

The Bible Isaiah 55:8 tells us, *"For my thoughts are not your thoughts, neither are your ways my ways, declares the Lord."* This is why practicing God's ways will be helpful, because they are not our ways. God really does have the answers and wisdom we need to live out His awesome plan for our lives.

So what's the next step? Let's pray.

**Prayer**

*Dear God, please help me to do things Your way. I know I can't do this on my own. I am going to need Your help, God. I want to experience Your peace and I want more than anything to please You, by living my life Your way. Thank you for helping me to be thankful, and please help me put Your words into practice. Amen.*

Next Step

The next step is to practice being thankful to God. Tell God what you are thankful for right now. Just say it, out loud. Do this several times a day. It is especially helpful to do this when you are doing something you would rather not be doing, like homework or chores.

Here's an example: just the other day, I had to clean the bathroom, which I wasn't looking forward to. So I said out loud, "Thank you, God, for giving me this bathroom to clean." Now you may laugh at this, but do you know what God did for me? As I was cleaning the toilet bowl and practicing being thankful, the Lord let me know that my heart used to be just as dirty as that toilet.

What does that mean? All those faulty thoughts I used to have about God and others polluted me with anger, bitterness, and resentment. Those bad thoughts were sin towards God and other people. It made my heart spiritually "dirty."

But God reminded me that He has cleansed my heart, and He impressed upon me the importance of continuing to come to Him every single day and spending time with Him, so that He can keep my heart clean. He does that by helping me forgive, and by helping me be thankful for everything in my life. God knows that even when we are practicing His ways, we still need His help, and He always wants to help us.

Just as the toilet cannot clean itself, we are not able on our own to clean sin out of our hearts and minds. No matter how much we practice, we will never be perfect. It is only Jesus who can wash away anything that could pollute our hearts and minds. God wants to keep us clean. He wants to fill us with peace, but it begins with us turning to Him.

Let's never take God for granted. Let's spend time with Him daily, and with His help, let's put His words into practice. And let's be very thankful that He does not expect us to be perfect!

# Busyness

When asked why they don't spend more time with God, many people will answer, "I'm too busy," or "I just don't have the time." This is a stumbling block, and it poses a problem for us.

Think about a typical week in your life. Most of us have to get up early in the morning, go to school or work, and after that, we may have homework or household chores to do, or other activities like sports, after-school clubs, music lessons, and so on. By the end of the day, we are exhausted. Included in this busy day we manage to stay connected with our friends--in person, or, more often, with devices: phones, tablets, iPads, computers, etc. These devices, though, with all their cool games and apps, make it easy for us to lose track of what little time we have left in the day. Before we know it, it's bedtime, and we start the whole routine all over again the next day.

Just as we want to stay connected with our friends and spend time with them, in spite of all the distractions in our lives, God wants to connect with us and spend time with us too. We get so busy, though, it's easy for us to forget about God.

God won't force us to spend time with Him. We are free to set our own schedules. But God longs to have a deep personal relationship with us. He patiently waits for us to make time for Him. Unfortunately, we sometimes put Him aside, and make Him wait a very long time. Usually this is also when we find ourselves stressed out, lacking peace, and not knowing how to "fix" the problems in our life.

This is something many people struggle with, so don't feel bad if you find yourself in this kind of situation. God does not want us to feel guilty. He just wants us to spend time with Him. If this is something you are dealing with, the following prayer may help.

### Prayer

*Dear Lord, I am sorry I have not made time for You. Please forgive me, Lord, and help me to better manage my schedule. Show me how You would like me to live my life, and help me make time for You every single day. Thank You, Lord Jesus. Amen.*

God often speaks to us in the quiet moments in our lives. But with all the distractions available to us, we are apt to avoid these quiet times. We have many fillers that can rob us of our opportunity to spend time with God. Fillers are things like watching TV, listening to music, or playing video games. All these things can steal precious time that we could be spending with God.

The idea of spending time alone with God can be intimidating. We may want to stay busy, to avoid being alone with God. Time spent alone with God is time away from the busyness of life. We may use that time to read the Bible and pray, but it can also be time just sitting there in the quiet, allowing God the time to clean our hearts and minds.

But what does this look like? It may sound a little scary, but don't fear time alone with God. We may be thinking God will punish us for something we've done wrong, or give us some harsh message that we don't want to hear. But there is no reason to be afraid of spending time with God. If we feel afraid of God Himself, it's only because we don't fully know Him yet.

Spending time with someone we don't know very well can make us feel uncomfortable. Think of your first day of school. You didn't know more than a few other kids; maybe you didn't know anyone at all. You didn't know what it was going to be like. I'll bet you were a little bit nervous.

But then you were able to meet some people, make friends, and see that it wasn't so bad after all. Well, God is way better than school! He loves us so much, He treats us better than anyone else. He will never do anything or say anything to hurt us. He only loves us and He always wants to help us.

The Bible 1 Kings 19:12 says, *"After the earthquake came a fire, but the Lord was not in the fire. And after the fire came a gentle whisper."*

God often speaks to us in whispers, and we can speak to Him the same way. Words spoken in whispers are often a shared secret. God whispers gentle, kind and loving things to us. He also gives us direction and helps us think about things in a new and different way. And we can share anything we want with Him. He is very safe, and He is the best one to share our deepest secrets with.

That's true even if those secrets are about something bad. In fact, especially if it's something bad. God will always help us with it, no matter how ashamed or embarrassed we feel. God will always let us know what is best for us.

These whispers with God are great blessings in our lives. Once we know how much God really loves us and wants to help us, we will discover that spending time with Him is the only way to get fear out of our lives, and to gain that incredible sense of peace God wants us to have.

If you have been afraid to spend time with God, or just haven't found time for God in your daily life, here are some prayers that may be helpful.

### *Prayer*

*Dear Lord, I want to spend time with You. Please reveal to me who You really are, and help me understand Your love, Lord. I do not want to be afraid of You. I am learning that You really are for me, and have created me for a special purpose. I am ready to find out what that purpose is. Please help me turn to You with all my heart. Amen.*

**Prayer**

*Dear God, forgive me for shutting You out by staying so busy all the time. I want to know who You really are, Lord. Please enter my heart and mind. I want You in my life. Help me let go of all the distractions and things I don't need in my life. Help me spend time with You in the quiet, Lord. I want to hear Your gentle voice. Amen.*

Next Step

Get quiet with God. Make some time for Him each day. You can do this anytime. Just go to a room all by yourself and shut the door, even if it has to be the bathroom or a closet. Remember, God is interested in you and your heart. He does not care what room you choose; He just wants to spend time with you. That's why the Bible states, *"When you pray, go into your private room, shut your door, and pray to your Father, who is in secret. And your Father, Who sees in secret, will reward you."* (Matthew 6:6 HCSB)

Once you're alone with God, say out loud, "Here I am, God; I am here to spend time with You." Then just sit in the quiet. You may want to have your Bible with you.

Why just sit there in the quiet? Well, it's good to talk to God; that's what we call prayer, and we should pray. But it's important to be quiet too, so that God can talk to us as well. God may not speak every time, but He will always fill us up with His love, peace and gentleness.

May you always know how much you mean to Him!

# Peace in the Quiet

I have learned over the years that I need to spend a lot of time with God. In fact, I couldn't write these books if I didn't spend time with Him. It's in my quiet time with God that He reveals what I need to write about. Otherwise I would have no clue what the books are supposed to be about!

One day, in the quiet time, our Lord spoke to me. He told me He needed to reveal some things to me, but He couldn't do it as long as I had my duties to perform as a wife and mom. I knew God was not asking me to leave my family; what He was telling me was that I needed to get away and spend an entire weekend alone with Him, with no distractions.

It was the first time the Lord placed on my heart to go away on a retreat. Retreats are periods when we set aside special time to be with God. Some people choose to do retreats at places called monasteries. A monastery is a community of monks who spend their lives in prayer and service to God. The monastery I went to also allows ordinary people to stay there for private retreats. So I stayed in the monastery's retreat house for an entire weekend.

At this particular monastery, the monks live in almost total silence. Except when they are praying, they rarely speak. They do that to help them concentrate on prayer and growing closer to God.

Jesus wanted his disciples to have this kind of quiet time with God too. The Bible Mark 6:31 tells us that on one occasion, *"because so many people were coming and going that [Jesus and his disciples] did not even have a chance to eat, He said to them, 'come with me by yourselves to a quiet place and get some rest.'"*

Jesus also needed solitude. In the Bible Luke 5:16 says, *"But Jesus often withdrew to lonely places and prayed."* The more time we spend with God in silence, then, the more we will notice Him working in our hearts and lives.

When I realized God wanted me to go on a retreat, I thanked Him for letting me know this was what I needed to do. I went on the retreat, and sure enough, God revealed something to me that I needed to make right. God was cleansing my heart, and He showed me that I had done something hurtful to someone years ago, that I had completely forgotten about.

The Lord reminded me of a disagreement I'd had with a very good friend of mine. She didn't share my opinion about some things that seemed important to me at the time. So I turned this person away and treated her badly. I felt offended by her, just because she didn't agree with me. I told my friend she had hurt my feelings. She said she was sorry and she asked me to forgive her. But I just couldn't do it. I felt hurt, offended, and angry. I let that friendship slip away. I have done the same sort of things to other people in my life, too. It became a bad habit.

This particular situation happened so many years ago, I had completely forgotten about it. I hadn't even thought about this person in years. But God reminded me of it, and He pointed out to me that He had never treated me the way that I had treated my friend. Even when I'd hurt His feelings by some of the bad choices I'd made in my life, God never turned away from me.

God showed me that it's never OK to disregard other people, to ignore their feelings, or to try to hurt them or punish them just because they've made us angry. Of course it's good to have boundaries. Sometimes we need to remove ourselves from unhealthy situations. But this was not always the case with some of the people that I've turned away from.

When I received this message, all I could say was, "Thank you, Jesus, for not treating me the way I have treated other people." I wrote my friend a letter of apology and I asked her to forgive me. And I made things right with the other people I had hurt as well. The Lord was showing me I didn't have to stumble over who people are, or what they believe, for me to accept them. And people do not have to agree with me in order for me to love them. God loves all of us all the time, no matter how badly we mess up, and no matter what mistakes we make. He always loves us. He is our example of what love is, and what love is all about.

The reason why I wanted to share this story with you is to show that we should never be afraid of spending time alone with God. This experience demonstrates how God helps us in the quiet times. Even when we have done something wrong, God only wants to help us gain more love and peace in our hearts. He is not out to get us, hurt us, or punish us. He may need to point some things out to us and help us change our path, but He does not expect us to do this alone. He is happy to help us, and He rejoices when we turn to Him. The Bible Proverbs 3:11-12 says, *"My son, do not despise the Lord's discipline, and do not resent his rebuke, because the Lord disciplines those he loves, as a father the son he delights in."*

The reason why God cares about us so much is that He wants us to be the world changers He created us to be. Once God teaches us and helps us understand better ways, He then uses us, and what He has taught us, to help others as well. This is why we can be thankful to God, and not be scared of spending time with Him in the quiet.

### Prayer

*Dear God, help me not be afraid to come to You in a quiet place. Please cast out all my fear, Lord, and help me turn to You. I am ready to live the life You want me to live and be all You created me to be. Thank You so much, Lord. Amen.*

# Jesus and the Holy Spirit

There is a well-known passage in the Bible that tells us just how much God loves us. Let's take a look at it. John 3:16 says, *"For God so loved the world that He gave his only son, so that whoever believes in Him should not perish, but have eternal life."*

That scripture is talking about Jesus, God's son. He came to the world to live among us as a human being: God literally in the flesh. God wanted us to be able to understand and relate to Him in a new way. God saw that we humans were making some pretty poor choices and doing some pretty bad things, like lying, stealing, cheating, and hurting others. These kinds of bad things are called sin. Jesus wanted to help us stop sinning, but He also wanted to create a way for us to be forgiven, and to forgive one another when we mess up. He wanted us to know His love for us, so that we could share His love with others. It made Jesus very sad to see people hurting each other. So He came to earth to teach us God's ways of doing things. He showed us how to live. And because Jesus Himself never sinned, He knew exactly how to help us!

Jesus knows sin affects all our lives, so He teaches us how to avoid sin. But Jesus also knows we're not perfect. He understands that there will be times when we fail, when we are confused, selfish, overwhelmed, and scared. So when we do sin, Jesus helps us move forward. He doesn't want us to be trapped in sin and guilt. Jesus is able to do all this because He was tempted by sin, just as we are. The difference is, He was able to say NO to it every time! So we can be sure His advice is good, true, and right. This is great news for us. It means that Jesus will help us no matter what situation we find ourselves in.

If we need help out of a sinful situation, which we all do, let's say this prayer together.

**Prayer**

*Dear Jesus, please forgive me for (name the sin). Please heal me, and the others who may have been hurt by this sin. Please help me to make better choices. Thank you, Jesus, for showing me a better way. Amen.*

So How is Jesus able to create for us a way out of sin? Let's explore this together. In the Bible Luke 9:22 tells us that Jesus once said to his followers, *"The Son of Man [Jesus] must suffer many things and be rejected by the elders, the chief priests, and the teachers of the law, and he must be killed and on the third day be raised to life."*

Let's think about that for a moment. Jesus was doing amazing things here on earth. He was healing people, performing miracles, even bringing people back to life, and all the while pointing the way back to God. So what went wrong? Why was Jesus put to death?

In spite of all the good things that Jesus was doing, there were some people who were very jealous of Him. They wanted to be in charge, and they wanted people to listen to them only.

It was an amazing time with Jesus here on earth. Many people were drawn to God's ways through Jesus' teachings and actions. Some leaders felt threatened by this. They became angry, and they came up with a plan to get rid of Jesus. His teachings questioned their way of doing things. They wanted to make Jesus suffer, as a warning to others not to question their ways. They even planned to murder Jesus.

Jesus knew all of this was going to happen, so that is why He told His friends about it early on. He wanted them to be prepared when it did happen. And sure enough, it happened just as Jesus said it would. He suffered and was killed by being nailed to a cross. And just as He promised, He also came back to life on the third day.

What does all this mean? When Jesus died on the cross, He took all of our sins with Him, so we no longer have to carry or be chained down by our sins. When Jesus came back to life, He forgave every sin we have ever committed. Any bad or evil thing we have done that goes against God's ways, He forgives. He also forgives anything we will ever do in the future, so when we mess up—and we all do—Jesus has already forgiven us for that too.

Now that doesn't mean that it's OK to sin, or that sin isn't harmful. Sin hurts us and those around us. Just because God loves us and forgives us does not mean we can go on acting badly on purpose. God wants to live with us forever and He wants to teach us better ways. But God is so good and so holy, He cannot live with sin. So sin poses a problem, and Jesus is the solution. He makes a way for you and me, who are imperfect, to live forever with God, who is perfect. Because of what Jesus did on the cross, we have continual forgiveness that never goes away.

I know this can be hard to understand. The Bible itself says, that no matter how hard we try, we can never fully grasp all of God's works:

*"I observed all the work of God and concluded that man is unable to discover the work that is done under the sun. Even though a man labors hard to explore it, he cannot find it; even if the wise man claims to know it, he is unable to discover it."* (Ecclesiastes 8:17 HCSB)

We cannot begin to understand how deep Jesus' love is for us. He loves us so much that He was willing to suffer terrible things here on earth, just so we could be close to Him and live with God forever!

The great news for us is that we do not have to be perfect or understand everything fully, in order to enjoy God's blessings. All we need to know is that because of Jesus, we can have an awesome personal relationship with God! And we can live out the beautiful plan God has for our lives here on earth, right here and now. Look at what Jesus said: *"The thief comes only in order to steal, kill and destroy, I came that they may have and enjoy life, and have it in abundance (to the full, till it overflows)."* (John 10:10 AMP)

So yes, Jesus suffered, died and rose again to give us life, and He wants us to enjoy that life. Let's remember the Bible verse in Ephesians 2:10: *"For we are God's handiwork, created in Christ Jesus to do good works, which God prepared in advance for us to do."*

Romans 8:11 puts it this way: *"If the Spirit of him who raised Jesus from the dead is living in you, He who raised Christ from the dead will also give life to your mortal bodies because of his Spirit who lives in you."*

God loves us so much, He never wants to be separated from us, either during our lives here on earth or after we die. We are truly blessed that Jesus cares so much about us.

After Jesus came back to life, He visited His friends. When they saw Jesus alive, they realized the truth of what He had told them before— that He had to die, but that He would be resurrected; in other words, that He would come back to life, just as He had said He would. And they realized that this was a sign from God, that through Jesus' life, death and resurrection, sin and death no longer have any power over us.

We also know from the Bible that after He rose from the dead, Jesus stayed on the earth for a little while. When His work here was done, Jesus left the earth, to return to God in Heaven, anointing His disciples to continue the work He had started.

Although Jesus physically left the earth, He did not abandon us. He is still with us today.

How can that be? The Bible John 14:26-27 tells us. When it was time for Jesus to physically leave the earth, Jesus told His disciples that He had to return to His father in Heaven. But, He added, *"The Advocate, the Holy Spirit, whom the Father will send in my name, will teach you all things and he will remind you of everything I have said to you. Peace I leave with you; my peace I give you. I do not give to you as the world gives. Do not let your hearts be troubled and do not be afraid."*

So when Jesus returned to the Father in Heaven, God gave us His Holy Spirit to live in us. We ourselves, then, are literally God's home! God's Holy Spirit dwells in us today. The Bible says, *"Don't you yourselves know that you are God's sanctuary and that the Spirit of God lives in you?"* (1 Corinthians 3:16 HCSB)

As Jesus explained to His disciples in John 14:26-27, the Holy Spirit's job is to teach us, guide us, and remind us of all Jesus' teachings. That is why the Holy Spirit is also known as the Comforter and the Counselor. It is He who counsels us and helps us make better choices. And when we are upset about our problems, He comforts us. The Holy Spirit is also known as the Helper, because He helps us in our daily lives. And since He lives in us, He knows about everything going on in our lives.

The Holy Spirit does so much for us. This truly is a comfort, because often we think we have to do everything on our own, but that is not so. We just have to let God know we want Him in our lives, and His Spirit will get to work helping us every day of our lives. Remember, He won't force us into anything, so it's our job to let God know we want and need Him in our lives. But there is something very comforting about knowing we will never walk alone. No matter what we are going through, God is going through it with us. He already knows exactly what is needed to help.

If you are ready and would like to begin your very own relationship with Jesus and be filled to overflowing with the Holy Spirit, the following prayer may help.

### Prayer

*Dear Jesus, please forgive me for all my sins. I know I have done things that were wrong. I believe You are God's son, and I believe You died and came back to life for me. I want to live with You forever, Lord, and I want to experience Your peace. Please enter my heart and my life, and fill me to overflowing with your Holy Spirit, Lord. Help me to live out the plan You have for me. Thank You so much, Jesus, for everything You have done. Amen.*

Now just take a moment to be with the Lord. This is truly the most important relationship we will ever have.

Next Step

The next step is to start spending time with God on a regular basis. With any relationship, the more time we spend with someone, the better we get to know them. Well, the same is true for God. Just because we can't see Him doesn't mean He isn't there. He speaks to us through His Holy Spirit.

The Holy Spirit will always speak to our hearts and guide us in the way we should go, but we need to make time for God, so that we can hear His Holy Spirit speak to us in the quiet.

It is also a good idea to read the Bible regularly. The Bible is full of God's teachings, and reading His words will Help us know just how much He truly does love us. We will also find good advice in the Bible on how to better handle difficult situations God's way.

No feeling will ever come close to the peace God has for us. God does not want us to be afraid of spending time with Him. He wants us to have peace. And we can, but it all starts with inviting Jesus into our hearts and lives. God wants us right where we are. Our past does not matter; it does not matter where we come from, or who are parents are, or what we have done. God wants us because He loves us. Don't allow anything to stop you from getting close to Him.

# It's Time To Tell the Truth

We have learned so far that reading our Bible and putting it into practice is very good for us, but why? Sure, the Bible is full of God's words and teachings, but it is so much more than simply a "how-to book." Yes, it does teach us how to live a peaceful life, and how to be the world changers God created us to be, but the Bible goes far beyond that. It is God's living, breathing words to us. The words Jesus spoke while He was here on earth are in the Bible. The messages He spoke to people through the Holy Spirit are in the Bible.

God has always wanted a relationship with us. He has spoken to us, and even through us, ever since the creation of the world. The Bible reveals God's love for us. His word is timeless, because God is forever. Everything He has said applies to our lives today. And since God is perfect, it is impossible for Him to lie. So when we read the Bible, we are reading the absolute truth. The truth does not change. What was true 200, or 2000 years ago is still true today.

It's very important for us to discuss this, because once we invite Jesus in and ask Him to fill us with the Holy Spirit, the Holy Spirit will reveal His truth to us. Jesus has told us: *"When the Spirit of Truth comes, He will guide you into all the Truth. He will not speak on His own but will tell you what He has heard. He will tell you about the future. He will bring me glory by telling you whatever he receives from me. All that belongs to the Father is mine; this is why I said, the Spirit will tell you whatever he receives from me."* (John 16:13-15 NLT.)

Please take a moment to reflect on this scripture. Ask God right now to reveal the truth to you. The Holy Spirit will always reveal to us what we need to know. He will tell us what He hears from God. The Holy Spirit is constantly connected to God and when God speaks, the Holy Spirit will tell us, committing Himself to the personal relationship God wants with us. God speaks to us through the Holy Spirit, so that we can be everything God created us to be.

How do we hear the Holy Spirit? The best way I can answer that question is by sharing something that once happened to me. One day as I was praying to God and just spending time with Him, God put on my heart that I needed to go to the bank and take out ten dollars in cash. I didn't know why, so I wasn't sure at first if I should go. But when I thought about not going to the bank, I lost my sense of peace. I wanted to keep my peace, so I went to the bank and took out ten dollars. I didn't know what to do with it or why I needed it, so I just stuck it in my wallet and went about my day.

One of the things I needed to do that day was go to the grocery store. I got everything I needed and headed to the checkout line. The person in line in front of me was an older lady. I happened to notice the things she was buying, because there wasn't much in her basket. She had celery, onions, carrots and milk; maybe one more item, but that was it. The reason I noticed this was because my cart was full of snacks and sweets and meats. It struck me that she was buying the bare minimum: no snacks, no chips, nothing fun to eat. She was buying only what she needed to live on.

As she went to pay, the lady gave the cashier a card that looked like it was some kind of program card, like food stamps or something similar. The cashier swiped the card, and told the woman that there wasn't enough money on the card to cover her items. The woman seemed surprised, and said that there should have been ten dollars on the card. But the cashier said no, there wasn't, so the woman would not be able to buy her groceries.

I immediately knew at that point that the ten dollars the Lord wanted me to take out of the bank was meant for this woman! I pulled out the $10 bill and gave it to the cashier for her. Because of that ten dollars, she was able to buy all of her groceries. She looked directly at me and she said, "May God bless you, He will always provide."

Now I am not telling you this story to show what a good person I am. I wanted to share this story with you to show you how good God is. I had no idea why the Holy Spirit wanted me to get ten dollars from the bank, but He knew why. I certainly didn't know that I would even be seeing this woman, much less what her situation was, but God knew. God is the one who planned that whole day out. He knew what that lady needed and what time she would be at the store. He chose to help her through me. And when He did, she blessed me right there in the store. She was also a reminder that God really will always provide for us.

I also wanted to share this with you to show that we shouldn't be afraid and think, well, what if I can't hear the Holy Spirit? No matter when the Holy Spirit chooses to speak to us, we will always know when a message comes from the Lord. We will sense what is the right thing to do. Do not get caught up in how God will speak, just have faith and know that He will. God knows how to reach us, and He knows how to speak to us because He created us. He truly knows what we need and when we need it. That is why having a relationship with God is so important. We can always trust God to tell us the truth and to give us the information we need for our lives. It's truly amazing how God wants to help us and be with us, but for that to happen, we need to make time for God.

If you would like to allow God to use you to be a blessing to someone, let's say a prayer together and ask God to do that.

### Prayer

*Dear God, thank You for always knowing what we need and when we need it most. Help me not to live my life only thinking about myself. Please use me, Jesus, to be a blessing to other people, so that we can all experience Your love. Amen.*

Now let me say a little bit more about reading the Bible. Some people look at the Bible and think, "Oh, it's so long, how would I ever be able to read all that?" Well, you don't have to read it all in one night, or one week, or even one month. There's no time limit. The awesome thing about God's Word is that it puts truth in us every time we read it, no matter how much or how little we read. So even if we just read a few sentences from the Bible, that still means more of God's truth going into us, than if we hadn't read it at all.

Sometimes we may also think, "Well, I know someone who has read the Bible, so I'll just learn about it from them." That can lead to problems, however, because all people are imperfect. They may misunderstand what they read, and they don't know what God wants to do in our life. So they may tell us things they think we ought to know, but it may not be God's truth for our life. They might unknowingly put their own spin on the truth, or tell us a half-truth, or even a straight-out lie. Even if they honestly believe what they're telling us, they may be distorting God's truth, without realizing it. We can't be sure, and that is the danger.

Now I'm not saying that we should never talk or listen to other people about God or the Bible. My point is, we don't want to only believe what other people tell us about God, without going to God and reading the Bible ourselves. We can listen to what others tell us about God, and we can let that inspire us to learn what the Bible says. God will show us what He wants us to learn. We can trust the Holy Spirit to lead us and guide us into the truth. No one else has the ability to do what the Holy Spirit does. Let's remember the scripture above, *"When the Spirit of Truth comes, He will guide you into all the Truth. He will not speak on His own but will tell you what He has heard. He will tell you about the future. He will bring me glory by telling you whatever he receives from me. All that belongs to the Father is mine; this is why I said, the Spirit will tell you whatever he receives from me."* (John 16:13-15 NLT)

Well, what about when we go to church? Don't they read the Bible there? Shouldn't we be able to trust our church leaders to tell us about God?

Church can be a great place to worship God in company with other people, and to read our Bibles together. It can also be very good to listen to a wonderful message about God. However, we shouldn't rely on that alone. Good leaders of the church will always advise us to ask the Holy Spirit to reveal the truth to us. Good leaders will also encourage us to read the Bible for ourselves and take time to pray and ask God about what we have read and heard. If we don't go to God ourselves, we run the risk of being led astray, and that can cause all kinds of problems in our lives.

In the Bible John 8:31-32, Jesus says to a group of his followers, *"If you hold to my teaching, you are really my disciples. Then you will know the truth, and the truth will set you free."* What did Jesus mean by that? When Jesus asks us to hold to His teachings, He means we need to put His teachings into practice in our daily lives. The only place to find His teachings is in the Bible, and the Holy Spirit will reveal the truth to us.

Once we start doing what Jesus asks us to do, we will start to experience His peace more and more. And when that happens, we learn that God's way truly is the only way to keep our peace in all types of situations. God's way is always truth, and His ways are what give us peace. When we are at peace, we are set free. Free to serve God, free to live out His plan for our lives, and free to be everything He created us to be.

If we don't personally know God, and just try to learn about Him through someone else, we will never completely learn the fullness of God's truth. But when we learn God's truth for ourselves, we allow the Holy Spirit to work in us and help us. We know God is with us, and that enables us to experience God in a very direct, and real way. Let's take a look at Philippians 4:6-7, which talks about this: *"Do not be anxious about anything, but in every situation by prayer and petition with thanksgiving present your requests to God. And the peace of God which tran-*

scends all understanding will guard your hearts and your minds in Christ Jesus."

So when we turn to God ourselves by prayer and petition and thanksgiving, we receive a deep sense of peace, and God protects our hearts and minds from being led astray.

Let's turn to God right now. Here is a prayer to help.

**Prayer**

*Dear God, I want to know You personally, and I want to experience Your love and peace. Please help me by filling me up with Your Holy Spirit, and please lead me into Your truth. Amen.*

Next Step

Pick up your Bible and ask the Holy Spirit to reveal God's truth to you. Ask God to help you fully understand His words and what it is He would like you to know. Then open your Bible and start reading. You can read anywhere in the Bible, you do not have to start at the beginning, since all of God's Word is truth. In fact, the Holy Spirit may even guide you as to where to open your Bible and start reading.

"Make them holy by your truth; teach them your word, which is truth." (John 17:17 NLT.)

May you be blessed with God's truth as it pours over you and gives you peace!

# Peace Stealers

So far in this book we have discussed many things about God and peace. We understand that peace is key to revealing who God made us to be. Peace is most certainly something we want to experience. We also know that losing peace leads to bad emotions, like stress, frustration, fear, and anxiety. We have discussed how to receive peace from God. So what else is there to know?

Unfortunately, there are things in the world that try to take our peace away. I call them "peace stealers." Peace stealers can be thoughts, situations, or even people. They can be anything that shifts our focus away from God and onto other things. Peace stealers can lead us into sin, by getting us to focus on things that would cause us to forget about God and His plan for our lives. Peace stealers never want what's best for us.

Remember, we can become world changers when we keep our focus on God. When we live out God's plan for our lives, it helps our whole world. We know when we spend time with God, He can use us in mighty ways to do great things. But the enemies of God don't want this. They put obstacles in our way, like problems that we can't see a way to fix or overcome. Peace stealers may even create situations that sound appealing, but are really not good for us. We may think we would love to get involved in these situations, only to realize later that we have made the mistake of going our own way, instead of God's. These pesky peace stealers want us to forget all about God's plan, and they can be very sneaky.

Fortunately, we have a firm foundation we can rely on! We have learned to thank God for everything that comes our way, good or bad, we have invited Jesus into our hearts and lives, and we know we can trust God, because the Holy Spirit is leading us into truth. We are reading and praying our Bible, and putting His words into practice. Hopefully, we are spending quiet time with God too.

So then, how can these peace stealers take our peace from us? The good news is they can't, unless we allow them to.

As Jesus tells us in the Bible John 10:10, *"The thief comes only to steal and kill and destroy. I have come that you may have life, and have it to the full."* So Jesus isn't going to steal anything from us. He is going to give us peace, and life, and He is going to help us enjoy our life now and forever. We can love who He created us to be.

So how do we avoid and defeat these peace stealers? First, remember how they work. These pesky stealers try to shift our focus away from God by using things that tempt us to go our own way, and to forget about following God. Their ultimate goal is to stop us from getting close to God, because they know God's plans for us are powerful.

One way peace stealers do this is by trying to get us to believe lies. Lies like, we need some material thing to make us happy. Or that we have to make a quick decision about important things in our life, without going to God in prayer first. The truth is, we don't need physical things to make us happy, and we don't have to make impulsive decisions. We don't have to give into any kind of pressure. We are all capable of saying, "I need time to pray about this."

Don't forget, peace stealers are powerless by themselves. They cannot stop us from following God. That's why the Bible James 4:7 says, *"Submit yourselves, then, to God. Resist the devil and he will flee from you."* So the only way peace stealers can truly steal our peace is if we believe their lies instead of turning to God and His truth.

Remember the story about my friend that I had not forgiven for many years? That was the enemy's trap that I fell into. When I first became angry at her, I had some pretty bad thoughts about her. Thoughts like, "She will never support me. I should have friends who always agree with me." I was afraid I would get hurt if my friends didn't agree with me or share my opinions. It took me a long time to realize that these thoughts were false and destructive.

Remember, the Holy Spirit will lead us into absolute truth. The Bible states, *"since the weapons of our warfare are not worldly, but are powerful through God for the demolition of strongholds. We demolish arguments and every high-minded thing that is raised up against the knowledge of God, taking every thought captive to obey Christ."* (2 Corinthians 10:4-5 HCSB)

What this means for our lives is that if we find we are often having thoughts that seem to be affecting our peace, we can give those thoughts to Jesus. We can ask Him to remove those false or negative thoughts and to help us understand His truth. He will always help us overcome. Here is a prayer to help us do that.

**Prayer**

*Dear God, I nail every lie I have been believing about You, myself, and others to the Cross of Jesus. Forgive me for believing these lies, and thank you so much, God, for covering me with Your truth. Amen.*

Peace stealers cannot make us believe lies. We get to choose what we want to believe, but it is only when we turn to God and give our thoughts to Him that we will learn the whole truth. When I was angry at my friend, I should have gone to God right away and asked Him for help. He would have guided me through that situation, but I chose to listen to fear and believe lies instead. Because of it, I lost a really good friend. But God was able to help me turn away from all those lies. He cleaned my heart, and I apologized to God and my friend. I hadn't even known I was believing lies, until I received the truth, and that is what set me free from all the anger and hurt that was in my heart.

Jesus knows what He is doing, and He knows how to lead us out of any trap we may fall into. We will not be able to overcome the enemy on our own, but fortunately, we are not on our own. The Bible tells us in 1 Corinthians 6:17 that *"whoever is united with the Lord is one with him in Spirit."* It also says, *"You, dear children, are from God and have overcome them, because the one who is in you is greater than the one who is in the world."* (1 John 4:4)

If you are struggling now with damaging, hurtful thoughts, let's turn to God for help and say a prayer together.

### Prayer

*Dear God, I have been struggling with certain thoughts. I submit them to You now. Please lead me into Your truth, and show me how You want me to handle this situation. Thank You, Jesus. Amen.*

Next Step:

If you are struggling with difficult emotions, you can look them up in the back of your Bible. There will be a list of scriptures you can turn to, that will help you deal with that particular problem.

I also have written a book for young people, *Your Feelings and What God Says About Them*, that you may find helpful. It is an A-to-Z guide that explains how to handle many troublesome emotions God's way.

With God's help, we can overcome anything the enemy puts in our path. And when we do mess up and fall into sin, God will help us out of it. He may not take all our problems away, and He may teach us something from our experience, but once we learn the truth, we won't make the same bad choices again.

The Bible says it this way: *"I can do all things through Christ who strengthens me."* (Philippians 4:13 NKJV)

God will always give us the strength to overcome anything that stands in our way of living out His plan for our lives. God really does want to see us succeed. He is for us and He loves us. He just waits patiently for us to ask Him to step in. As Jesus tells us in the Bible, *"I have told you these things so that in me you may have peace. In this world you will have trouble. But take heart! I have overcome the world."* (John 16:33)

It's true, Jesus has seen it all. He has overcome every sin that anyone could ever commit, and He has chosen to cover us and protect us, so that nothing we do, no matter how bad, will ever separate us from God. God will always help us; all we have to do is ask.

Let's turn to God once again in prayer.

### Prayer

*Dear God, thank You for helping me turn to You with all my heart. I need Your help, Lord. I cannot overcome the enemy on my own. I need You and Your Holy Spirit to help me live out Your plans for my life. Thank You for making me courageous and for helping me live a fearless life, God, so that I can be all You created me to be. Amen.*

# A Gift For You

Many of us are very thankful for everything Jesus has done for us. The more we learn about God, the more grateful we become. His truth fills us with joy and He helps us live out the awesome plan He has for us. After a while, though, we may stop and think, wait a second -- we don't deserve any of this; we're not good enough! And so we start trying to do all sorts of things to pay God back for His goodness. We try to earn His love instead of receiving it as a gift.

God has so much overwhelming love for us that we can never do enough to earn it or deserve it. It is impossible. Yet for some reason we sometimes find it difficult to accept this truth. We want to somehow repay God for His blessings. This is a dangerous way to think. What often happens is, we get stuck thinking that we have to do certain things to make God happy. The truth is, God does all these good things for us not because we deserve it, but simply because He loves us.

Why is that so hard for us to accept? Maybe it's because of how the world works. The world's way is to compete for everything. We are rewarded for how well we perform, and things are taken away from us when we don't do well. So we always feel that we have to do better, and be better. Sometimes we feel as if we need to be perfect.

From a very young age we are taught to compete with other people. It's not enough to be good; we have to win. And even when we do win, we are afraid of losing next time. So we quickly learn that the things of this world must be earned. And even when we get something, it can be taken away from us, or get lost or stolen. Because the world works this way, many of us think this is how God operates too, but it's not. Remember, Jesus said that He does not give as the world gives.

How does God give? It's hard to fully understand, because we have nothing on earth to compare it to. We must turn to God and His Word to see what He has to say to us about this.

The Bible states, *"For God is working in you, giving you the desire and the power to do what pleases Him."* (Philippians 2:13 NLT) This relates to one of God's greatest gifts to us. God wants us to understand that we cannot earn anything from Him. He knows if we try to work to earn His gifts, we will work ourselves into a frenzy that would never end. He tells us, it's not about us; it is the Lord who works in us! The works we try to do on our own will fail, because it is the work that God does in us and through us that matters. God, then, totally relieves us of any pressure to perform. God knows we cannot do it on our own; we cannot fix our problems all by ourselves, and God does not expect us to. He just wants us to invite Him in so that He can help us be all He created us to be.

This is also known as God's gift of grace. The Apostle Paul writes, *"But to each one of us grace was given according to the measure of Christ's gift."* (Ephesians 4:7 NKJV) Since God has made each of us for a special purpose, He has given us gifts to help us live out His plan for our lives. These gifts are called gifts of grace. Grace is God's way of helping us, and blessing us with whatever we need, to do all the things He has planned for us to do. He never meant for any of us to do anything apart from Him. So the gifts He gives us are directly linked to God's plans and purposes for our lives.

This scripture also lets us know we cannot earn God's grace; God bestows His grace on us as a gift, not as a reward. This is very important to understand, so I'll say it again: there is nothing we can ever do to earn God's gifts—that's why they are gifts!

But what if we mess up? Will God take back His gifts? No! He won't. The Bible Romans 11:29 tells us that, *"For God's gifts and his call are irrevocable."* In other words, God never withdraws His gifts once they are given, and He does not change His mind about the gifts He has given us, no matter how many mistakes we make.

That's right—no matter what, God never takes His gifts back! God created us for a purpose, and He never changes His mind about it — that's what "irrevocable" means. His call to us and His gifts for us are forever! God treats us very differently, then, from how the world treats us.

The Bible 1Peter 4:10 says, "*Each of you should use whatever gift you have received to serve others, as faithful stewards of God's grace in its various forms.*"

We are also told that, "*there are different kinds of gifts, but the same Spirit distributes them. There are different kinds of service, but the same Lord.*" (1 Corinthians 12:4-5.)

God has more than enough gifts for us, and for everyone else too. His Word lets us know we all have a job to do, but He does it through us and in us. He also has more than enough grace and goodness for all of us. And when God works through us, it becomes apparent that only God could do these things; we cannot do them on our own.

This is very helpful to understand, and it can make all the difference in the world if we can truly begin to see the people around us as God's gift to the world. People are God's creative solution to problems our world has. If we know and understand that God is working through other people, that will help us get out of the worldly way of thinking, which often sees other people as rivals or enemies that we have to compete with or defeat. We do not have to "beat" people at anything, because God made each one of us for a special purpose, which is unique and different from anyone else's purpose. He didn't make two people for the same purpose, and then sit back and watch to see which one is better. There is no competition among us, in God's eyes.

Think about it—there is no one else exactly like you! Even twins that look identical still have different personalities. That's why the Bible tells us in Ephesians 4:11-13, *"So Christ himself gave the apostles, the prophets, the evangelist, the pastors and teachers, to equip his people for works of service, so that the body of Christ may be built up until we all reach unity in the faith and in the knowledge of the Son of God and become mature, attaining to the whole measure of the fullness of Christ."*

This teaches us that God created each of us to help our world and each other. Did you catch that? Our gifts are never just for us alone. They are always meant to help build others up, but again it's God who works through us to do this. It is God who gives us exactly what we need, when we need it, to carry out His plans for our lives. He will let us know what and when something needs to be done, and then He will give us the tools and abilities we need to do it. We just have to be open to God's gifts and ask Him to lead us.

God loves us all so much that when He gives us His gifts, they will always help other people too. The gifts of grace are given to us so that God can work through us to make our world a better place.

The Bible says, *"Every good and perfect gift is from above, coming down from the Father of the heavenly lights, who does not change like shifting shadows."* (James 1:17)

This is awesome news, because God promises us He will do what needs to be done, and we know that if God says so, we can believe Him!

If you are ready, and would like to receive the gifts God has for you, the following prayer may help.

**Prayer**

*Dear God, please enter my heart and life and fill me to overflowing with the Holy Spirit. Please do in me whatever You need to do, so that You may work through me to make our world a better place. Thank You so much for never leaving me on my own. Amen.*

Next Step

We often forget it is God who works in us and through us. We may find ourselves in stress and full of anxiety because we are messing up and not sure what we are supposed to do at times. If we find ourselves in this situation, let's take the pressure off ourselves and turn our focus back to God, remembering it is He who will do the work, not us. If we do not feel led to do anything specific at the moment, then let's take that time to get to know God better, by spending some time with Him in the quiet. He will always let you know what the next step is.

Praying the following scripture and saying it out loud may also be helpful.

*"And I am certain that God, who began the good work within you, will continue his work until it is finally finished on the day when Christ Jesus returns."* (Philippians 1:6 NLT)

### Prayer

*Thank you, God, for reminding me it is You who works in me and through me. I know You will do everything You need to do to finish the work You have begun. I trust You to do what needs to be done, and if there is anything You want me doing in the meantime, please let me know. Amen.*

Now relax and trust God—you are His gift to our world in need!

# Conclusion

There is so much peace we can have in our lives. There is a place we all fit in, and an amazing plan for all of us. God has everything all worked out for us; He is just waiting for us to take that next step and come to Him. God wants what's best for us and He wants to give us amazing gifts because He loves us. We truly can be everything God created us to be.

Jesus looked at them and said, *"With man this is impossible, but with God all things are possible."* (Matthew 19:26)

God really can do amazing things. The more we practice being thankful, whether with big or little things, the more we will be able to be thankful always, even during hard times.

Turning our prayers into thankful prayers shifts our focus and perspective back to God. Saying prayers of thanks will help us open our hearts to trust God. Let's look for a moment at Philippians 4:6-7 in the Bible, *"Do not be anxious about anything, but in every situation by prayer and petition with thanksgiving present your requests to God. And the peace of God which transcends all understanding will guard your hearts and your minds in Christ Jesus."*

I want to use an example to help us understand this scripture. Think about a circle; a fully completed circle is closed, right? Nothing can get in that circle and nothing can get out. Now think of a half circle. A half circle, or semicircle, is wide open. It's not closed, so things can come in and go out. We are going to use this circle example to explore one more thing about thankfulness.

Let's look at the above scripture again: *"in everything by prayer and petition with thanksgiving present your requests to God."* When we pray, we are turning to God. When we make a petition, that means we are asking God for help with something. Here's an example: "Dear God, please help me pass my test."

Do you see something missing there? There is no "thanksgiving"—no thankfulness—in this prayer. So we have only done two of the three things mentioned in the scripture.

That doesn't mean this is a bad prayer, of course. It's never bad to ask God for help. But it's an incomplete prayer; it's like a half circle. Without the thankfulness part, our prayer is not complete.

Does that matter? Sure. Depending on what we are going through, those pesky peace stealers may try to get us to focus on how bad our problem is. They can get into our thoughts and feelings because we only have a half circle. They may put lies in our mind and make us wonder, is God really going to help me or not? Will He say yes or no to my prayer?

When we simply ask God for help, then, there is still room for fear and doubt to creep in, because our circle is not yet complete. If we leave our prayer that way, we may be tempted to fret over our problems and worry, even though we should be feeling comfort in knowing that God is going to help us. When we complete the prayer by adding thankfulness to it, we close the circle, so nothing bad can get in. We will have a full measure of peace, without fear or doubt. We are able to close the circle to keep those peace stealers out.

Let's take that earlier, incomplete prayer, and see what it would look like if we complete it with thankfulness.

### Prayer

*Dear God, please help me pass my test, and thank you for whatever happens, because I know you have a great plan for my life. Amen.*

Do you see the difference? We are still letting God know we need His help, so the prayer and petition parts are still there, but we are also thanking Him for the results, no matter what happens. This prayer leaves us in a state of total trust and peace. Even if we don't pass the test, we know God will work things out for us.

By thanking God, we are showing that we already know we have His help, regardless of how things turn out. They may not go our way, but we can be confident that God knows what He is doing. He knows the plan, so we can rest, and not worry, because God's got this in the bag!

Perhaps you are dealing with a problem of some kind right now. Let's take a moment, then, to say a prayer with all the components mentioned in Paul's letter.

### Prayer

*Dear God, please help me (state what it is you need). Thank you for always knowing and doing what is best in all my situations and problems. Amen.*

Now we will have peace, because we know that it's in God's hands, not ours.

The Bible also tells us that praying is not simply a matter of repeating some particular words. Jesus explained to His followers that when we pray, we should not think that whether God hears us depends on how many words we say. There is no need for us to go on "babbling," as some people did in Jesus' day. Jesus said, *"Do not be like them, for your Father knows what you need before you ask Him."* (Matthew 6:8.) Even before we pray, then, God already knows what needs to be done. So when we pray, we should not simply give God a "wish list" of things we want, but we should offer prayers of thanks. Offering prayers of thankfulness is God's will for us, and His ways always bring us peace.

How can we remember to do this? At some point in our lives, most of us have heard our parents or some other adult tell us to always say "please" and "thank you." Well, we can say "please" and "thank you" to God too. When we pray to God, we often start by saying something like, "God, please": "God, please help me do such and such," "God, please help me with this or that."

Generally, we only say "thank you" after someone has given us something or done something nice for us. But we need to remember, that's the way the world works. God does not give as the world gives, so our response needs to be different too.

God has already done lots of things for us, so we can already be thankful every time we pray. We don't need to wait to say "thank you" to God; we can and should start thanking Him right away. So our prayers may begin to look more like this: "God, thank you for helping me with such and such." "God, thank you for helping me do this or that." Such prayers of thanks set us up for much more peace, and we will gain a greater trust in God.

I'd like to leave you with just one more example of putting this teaching into practice. It happened while I was writing this conclusion. At the time, my daughter and I were in the middle of a major project of redecorating her bedroom. We were moving furniture and setting up new things. It was a lot of work, but we were having fun together.

At one point, my daughter's humidifier was in the way, so I moved it, and all of a sudden water started pouring out from the bottom all over the floor. My first instinct was to grumble and complain. I didn't want to deal with a humidifier just then; we wanted to decorate her room. But instead I thought, God knows what He is doing. This is happening for a reason; I know something good will come out of this.

My daughter scrambled to get towels and a bucket. All the while, water was still pouring out of the humidifier. But I thought, "This has to stop eventually—there isn't that much water in there." So I figured we would just drain the humidifier and be done with it.

We really didn't want to take the humidifier apart, because we knew that would take extra time and work, and my daughter and I were already in the middle of decorating her room. But I kept reminding myself how important it is to be thankful and to understand this was happening for a reason. We did have to take the humidifier apart, and we found it to be dirty and slimy inside. It was really gross. YUCK!

So if that humidifier hadn't leaked, I never would have thought about how badly it needed cleaning. And my daughter, who uses the humidifier a lot, would have been breathing in bad air. It probably would have made her sick eventually. We both ended up thanking God for letting us know about how filthy the humidifier was inside, because we couldn't see the dirty air. But God did; He knew, and He let us know it too.

God can always see the things we can't. And He sees what's best for us, even when we don't. Because my daughter and I trusted and thanked God, things turned out well in the end, and we were able to keep our peace through the whole ordeal.

It does take practice to be thankful. When things don't go the way we'd hoped or planned, we are usually inclined to complain about it. But God uses these "inconvenient" problems for our good and for the benefit of others. He knows what He is doing. We can trust Him because He is good and always faithful. He really does care about us, far more than we can imagine.

We may not always understand at the time why something is happening, but we know that God does. What we think is a problem, may not be a problem at all. God can deal with the worst problems, and turn them into a major blessing for us.

Let's take this challenge together and start thanking God for everything that comes our way. And let's start praying prayers of thanks, now and throughout our lives.

**Prayer**

*Dear God, thank You for helping me be thankful every day. Thank You so much for teaching me how to have peace. And thank You so much for just being You. I love You, Lord. Amen.*

Always Remember:

*"Do not be anxious about anything, but in every situation by prayer and petition with thanksgiving present your requests to God. And the peace of God which transcends all understanding will guard your hearts and your minds in Christ Jesus."* (Philippians 4:6-7)

May God bless you with a very thankful life!

# Suggested Reading List

The Holy Bible

There is a book, *Battlefield Of The Mind*, by author Joyce Meyer, that I highly recommend. The topics she covers are so important that she's written separate versions of this book, for kids, teens and adults. All three are terrific.

Other Books by Julie Chapus

*Your Feelings and What God Says About Them*

*The Blame Game*

If you have found this book helpful, please leave us a message or comment at: Christforkidsministries.com. We'd love to hear from you.

Christ For Kids Team

www.ingramcontent.com/pod-product-compliance
Lightning Source LLC
Chambersburg PA
CBHW071741040426
42446CB00012B/2421